THE
CRISP & SIMPLE
COOKBOOK

Effortless Air Fryer Recipes for Crispy, Flavorful Meals Every Day

HENRY M. DIAZ

Copyright © 2025 HENRY M. DIAZ

All rights reserved. No part of this book may be reproduced in any form or by any electronic or mechanical means, including information storage and retrieval systems, without written permission from the author, except for the use of brief quotations in a book review. This book is a work of non-fiction. All views and opinions expressed are those of the author. The author has made every effort to provide accurate information, but does not assume any responsibility for errors or omissions.

DISCLAIMER

Before embarking on the flavorful journey of *The Crisp & Simple Cookbook*, please take a moment to review this important information.

GENERAL INFORMATION

The recipes and tips in *The Crisp & Simple Cookbook* are designed to inspire and simplify your cooking experience. While we've worked hard to provide accurate and practical advice, your results may vary depending on your choice of ingredients, cooking methods, and equipment. Don't hesitate to adjust recipes to fit your preferences and resources—cooking is as much about creativity as it is about following instructions!

HEALTH AND SAFETY

Cooking with an air fryer is convenient and enjoyable, but it's essential to keep safety in mind:

- Handle hot surfaces and heated equipment, like your air fryer, with caution.
- Follow your air fryer's user manual for proper operation and care.
- Use kitchen tools such as tongs or mitts to avoid burns or injuries.
- Always store perishable items safely to maintain freshness and prevent spoilage.

Be mindful of allergies or dietary restrictions when preparing meals. If you have specific health concerns or food sensitivities, review each recipe thoroughly before starting. Consult a healthcare provider or nutritionist if you're unsure about any ingredients or dietary adjustments.

By following these safety measures, you can enjoy a fun, stress-free cooking experience while savoring the crispy and delicious results!

NUTRITIONAL INFORMATION

The nutritional information provided for the recipes in *The Crisp & Simple Cookbook* is an estimate and may vary based on the ingredients, brands, and portion sizes you use. While we strive for accuracy, factors like preparation methods and substitutions may cause slight variations.

For precise nutritional guidance or tailored dietary needs, consider consulting a nutritionist or using tools such as food scales or nutritional analysis apps to customize the recipes to your requirements.

Now that you're prepared, it's time to dive into the world of air fryer cooking! Let's embrace the simplicity, creativity, and joy that comes with making delicious meals effortlessly. Here's to crispy, flavorful dishes that make every bite a celebration!

Happy cooking, and may your kitchen be filled with the aroma of success!

About the Author

Henry M. Diaz is a passionate culinary enthusiast and recipe innovator, dedicated to transforming the art of cooking into an approachable and flavorful experience. With a profound love for creating savory dishes that are both satisfying and simple, Henry has meticulously curated a collection of air fryer recipes that bring joy to the table and confidence to every home cook.

Henry's culinary journey is rooted in a desire to simplify cooking without compromising on taste or tradition. His recipes reflect years of dedication to perfecting techniques that celebrate the richness of savory flavors while embracing the ease of modern cooking methods.

As a self-taught chef, Henry understands the challenges faced by cooks of all skill levels. This insight has shaped his approach to *The Crisp & Simple Cookbook*—a guide designed to empower everyone, from beginners to seasoned chefs, to create delicious meals with minimal effort. His philosophy champions fresh ingredients, straightforward methods, and the magic of the air fryer as a versatile kitchen tool.

Driven by the belief that food is a unifying language, Henry's recipes are crafted to foster connection, inspire creativity, and celebrate the simple pleasures of sharing a meal. Whether you're preparing a quick breakfast for one, a hearty dinner for the family, or a show-stopping dish for guests, his recipes prioritize ease, flavor, and satisfaction.

In *The Crisp & Simple Cookbook*, Henry invites readers to discover the endless possibilities of air fryer cooking. Through thoughtfully crafted recipes, practical tips, and engaging instructions, this book celebrates the beauty of savoring crispy, flavorful meals that nourish the body and soul.

More than just a cookbook, it's a testament to the joy and warmth that comes from creating extraordinary dishes in the simplest of ways.

This book belongs to

_____
_____
_____
_____
_____
_____
_____

Eating well isn't about perfection; it's about giving your body the care it deserves, one delicious bite at a time.

How to Use This Cookbook

Welcome to *The Crisp & Simple Cookbook*! This book is your trusted companion for creating crispy, flavorful meals using the air fryer. Whether you're new to air fryer cooking or a seasoned enthusiast, this guide is packed with inspiration, practical tips, and delicious recipes to make your time in the kitchen fun, efficient, and satisfying. Here's how to get the most out of your journey through *The Crisp & Simple Cookbook*:

Start with the Basics

If you're just beginning your air fryer adventure or want to brush up on fundamentals, start by exploring the introductory chapters. These sections lay the groundwork for success, covering:

- Essential ingredients to keep in your pantry for air fryer recipes.
- Tips for selecting and maintaining your air fryer.
- Key techniques to ensure crispy, perfectly cooked meals every time.

Explore Recipes by Meal Type

The cookbook is thoughtfully organized into sections to help you find the perfect recipe for any occasion:

- **Breakfast Recipes:** Energize your mornings with options like crispy breakfast burritos, air-fried frittatas, and golden waffles.
- **Lunch Recipes:** Enjoy satisfying dishes such as savory wraps, crispy salads, and hearty soups all elevated with air fryer magic.
- **Dinner Recipes:** Find everything from quick weeknight meals to impressive dishes perfect for entertaining, including air-fried mains and sides.

Plan Your Week with Ease

Meal planning has never been simpler! This cookbook includes:

- Step-by-step guidance for creating a weekly meal plan featuring a variety of recipes.
- Tips for prepping ingredients ahead of time to make busy days stress-free.

- Suggestions for mixing and matching recipes to suit your preferences and schedule.

Many recipes include make-ahead and reheating instructions, so you can enjoy fresh, delicious meals even on your busiest days.

Understand the Recipe Format

Each recipe in *The Crisp & Simple Cookbook* is crafted to make air fryer cooking straightforward and enjoyable. Here's what you'll find:

- **Ingredients List:** A selection of easy-to-find, wholesome ingredients that maximize flavor.
- **Prep Time & Cook Time:** Clear time estimates to help you plan your cooking efficiently.
- **Step-by-Step Instructions:** Detailed, easy-to-follow guidance for perfect results.
- **Pro Tips:** Expert advice for optimizing flavor, adjusting recipes, or simplifying preparation.
- **Storage and Reheating Notes:** Tips for keeping leftovers fresh and reheating them to perfection.

Customize Recipes to Fit Your Style

Cooking is personal, and this cookbook encourages creativity. Feel free to:

- Substitute ingredients to suit your dietary preferences or taste.
- Experiment with different seasonings, proteins, or vegetables.
- Add your own flair to recipes, making them uniquely yours.

Prioritize Healthy Choices

Air frying is a healthier way to enjoy your favorite dishes, and this cookbook highlights ways to keep meals light yet satisfying. Throughout the book, you'll find:

- Tips for reducing oil without sacrificing crispiness.
- Simple ingredient swaps to boost nutritional value.
- Strategies for balancing indulgence and health in every meal.

Embrace the Special Features

Beyond recipes, *The Crisp & Simple Cookbook* is a resource for simplifying your cooking routine and embracing the joy of creating crispy, delicious dishes. Don't miss:

- **Meal Planning Tips:** Learn how to stock your kitchen efficiently, plan meals seamlessly, and save time during busy weeks.
- **Air Frying Essentials:** Master the techniques that make air fryer cooking a game-changer in the kitchen.

Troubleshooting Guide

Cooking isn't always perfect, but that's part of the adventure! Here are some tips to keep you on track:

- **Crispiness Concerns:** Learn how to adjust cooking times, temperatures, or ingredients to achieve perfectly crispy results.
- **Troubleshooting Recipes:** From uneven cooking to seasoning tweaks, this guide offers practical solutions to common challenges.

Tips for Hosting

Elevate your gatherings with air fryer recipes that are crowd-pleasers and easy to prepare:

- Explore dishes that can be made in advance and reheated effortlessly.
- Cater to dietary preferences with customizable recipes.
- Discover ways to serve meals that feel special without added stress.

Learn as You Go

Cooking with an air fryer is a skill that gets better with practice. If you're a beginner, start with simpler recipes and build confidence as you go. *The Crisp & Simple Cookbook* is designed to grow with you, encouraging you to explore, experiment, and embrace the joy of cooking.

Share the Experience

Food has a magical way of bringing people together. Whether you're cooking for yourself or sharing a meal with loved ones, this book celebrates the connection and warmth that come with every bite. Found a favorite recipe? Put your spin on it and share it with family and friends—it's the best way to spread the love for crispy, flavorful meals.

Enjoy the Journey

The Crisp & Simple Cookbook is more than just a collection of recipes; it's a celebration of the ease, flavor, and creativity that air fryer cooking brings to your kitchen. Whether you're whipping up a quick snack or preparing a feast, this book is here to inspire, guide, and delight you.

So, grab your air fryer, choose a recipe that excites you, and get ready to transform simple ingredients into extraordinary meals. Here's to enjoying every crisp, flavorful moment—let's get cooking!

Table of Contents

Introduction 15
    What's Inside: A Fresh Approach to Cooking 15
    Interactive and Engaging Recipes 15
    Why "Crisp & Simple"? 16

How to Start and Stick to Air Fryer Recipes 17
    Get to Know Your Air Fryer 17
    Start Simple, Start Small 17
    Build Your Confidence 18
    Embrace Meal Planning 18
    Make It a Habit 19
    Mix Things Up 19
    Celebrate Your Wins 19
    QUESTION 21

How to Start and Stick to crispy Recipes 23
    Foods to Eat for Better Health 23
        Lean Proteins: 23
        Vegetables: 23
        Whole Grains: 24
        Nuts and Seeds: 24
        Healthy Fats: 24
    Foods to Avoid (or Eat in Moderation): 24
        Processed Meats: 24
        Refined Carbohydrates: 25

Pre-Packaged Fried Foods: 25

Sugary Snacks and Sweets: 25

Excessive Use of Oil: 25

Key Tips for Healthy Air Fryer Cooking: 26

question 27

Meal Planning for Beginner Air Fryer Recipes 28

Step 1: Understand Your Air Fryer's Capabilities 28

Step 2: Keep It Simple at First 28

Step 3: Create a Balanced Meal Plan 29

Step 4: Prep Ingredients in Advance 29

Step 5: Keep a Shopping List Handy 30

Step 6: Experiment with Simple Recipes 30

Step 7: Be Flexible and Adjust 31

Step 8: Enjoy the Process 31

Conclusion 31

7-Day Air Fryer Recipe Meal Plan 32

Day 1: 32

Day 2: 32

Day 3: 33

Day 4: 34

Day 5: 34

Day 6: 35

Day 7: 35

Tips for Success: 36

7 Comprehensive Air Fryer Breakfast Recipes 38

Air Fryer Avocado Toast 38

Air Fryer reakfast Burrito 39

Air Fryer Egg Muffins 40

Air Fryer Banana Oatmeal Bites 41

Air Fryer French Toast Sticks 42

Air Fryer Sweet Potato Hash 43

Air Fryer Breakfast Quesadilla 44

Air Fryer Chicken Caesar Salad 46

Air Fryer Turkey and Cheese Sandwich 47

Air Fryer eggie Burger 48

Air Fryer Chicken Tenders with Sweet Potato Fries 49

Air Fryer Mediterranean Chicken Wrap 50

Air Fryer Grilled Cheese with Tomato Soup 51

Air Fryer Falafel with Tahini Sauce 52

7 Comprehensive Air Fryer Dinner Recipes 54

Air Fryer Lemon Herb Chicken Thighs 54

Air Fryer Salmon Fillets 55

Air Fryer Stuffed Bell Peppers 56

Air Fryer Shrimp Scampi 57

Air Fryer ucchini Fritters 58

Air Fryer Chicken Parmesan 59

Air Fryer eriyaki Salmon Bowl 60

Conclusion 61

INTRODUCTION

Welcome to the *Crisp & Simple Cookbook*! Whether you're a seasoned pro in the kitchen or just starting out, this cookbook is your go-to guide for making savory meals that are not only delicious but also easy to prepare. In this book, we will journey through a world of crisp, flavorful, and satisfying dishes that fit seamlessly into your daily life. Think of it as your culinary companion—one that will guide you through the exciting and rewarding world of savory recipes.

If you've ever wondered how to bring out the best flavors in your meals without spending hours in the kitchen or sacrificing your health, you're in the right place. This cookbook has everything you need to get started, stay on track, and be successful with your savory recipes lifestyle.

WHAT'S INSIDE: A FRESH APPROACH TO COOKING

The recipes here are simple yet packed with flavor. We'll explore meal planning, tips, and of course, recipes designed for breakfast, lunch, and dinner. The focus is on quality ingredients and methods that bring out the natural goodness of your food. Along the way, you'll discover that cooking savory meals doesn't have to be complicated—especially when you embrace modern tools like the air fryer!

Air frying has revolutionized the way we approach healthy, flavorful cooking. Gone are the days of deep frying, excess oil, and greasy meals. The air fryer allows you to achieve that perfect crispiness while keeping the dish light and healthy. Whether you're a first-timer or an air fryer enthusiast, this cookbook will show you how to take full advantage of this powerful appliance. You'll find classic savory recipes with a fresh twist, and learn how to adapt old favorites to make them quicker, easier, and more satisfying.

INTERACTIVE AND ENGAGING RECIPES

This book isn't just a collection of recipes; it's an invitation to explore. We'll walk you through each recipe step by step, from the preparation to the final, delicious result. Along the way, we'll offer tips, shortcuts, and ideas to make your cooking even more efficient and enjoyable. Plus, we'll keep things interactive. You'll find suggestions for variations, ways to customize your meals, and helpful reminders for how to keep your cooking routine on track.

Every recipe in this book has been carefully curated to give you the tools you need for success. Whether you're looking to start the day with a savory breakfast, prep a satisfying lunch, or create a dinner that's sure to impress, we've got you covered.

WHY "CRISP & SIMPLE"?

We named this book *Crisp & Simple* because we believe in the power of simplicity. In today's fast-paced world, no one has the time to spend hours in the kitchen, and yet we all crave meals that are flavorful and fulfilling. The beauty of savory cooking is that it doesn't require complicated techniques or a dozen ingredients. What it needs is the right balance of flavors, the right tools, and the right approach. We've taken the guesswork out of cooking and streamlined the process so you can focus on what matters most—enjoying your food.

As you flip through the pages of this book, you'll be inspired to embrace a new, refreshing approach to meal planning and cooking. You'll realize that savory meals can be both effortless and extraordinary, and you'll be excited to share these delicious creations with those you love.

So, are you ready to start your savory cooking adventure? Grab your air fryer, your favorite ingredients, and let's dive in! The *Crisp & Simple Cookbook* is here to make cooking an experience you'll look forward to every day.

Let's get cooking crispy, simple, and full of flavor!

HOW TO START AND STICK TO AIR FRYER RECIPES

Starting something new can feel both exciting and a little intimidating, especially when it comes to cooking. If you're new to air frying, it's normal to feel unsure about how to get started, or even how to make it a lasting part of your routine. But don't worry—I've got you covered. The goal of this chapter is to help you get comfortable with your air fryer, build confidence, and make air frying a consistent and enjoyable part of your cooking lifestyle.

Let's dive in and take it step by step.

GET TO KNOW YOUR AIR FRYER

Before we get into the recipes, it's important to get to know your air fryer. I know it might seem like just a gadget in your kitchen, but your air fryer is about to become one of your best friends. Whether you have a simple model or one with all the bells and whistles, the basics are the same: air fryers use hot air to cook food quickly and crisply, giving you that perfect crunch without the need for a ton of oil. It's kind of like magic, but real.

Take a few minutes to read through the instruction manual that came with your air fryer. I know, manuals aren't always the most exciting read, but trust me, they can give you a lot of valuable insight into your specific model's features. Get familiar with the temperature settings, cooking times, and safety precautions. Some air fryers have presets for common foods (like fries, chicken, or fish), which makes it easier to get started.

START SIMPLE, START SMALL

When you're first starting out, it's best to begin with simple recipes. Don't dive into complex dishes just yet—give yourself room to experiment and get comfortable. The beauty of air frying is that even simple recipes come out delicious, and you'll quickly see how versatile this appliance can be.

Start with familiar, easy-to-make foods that you already enjoy. Try making air fryer French fries or crispy chicken wings. These are easy to make and require little prep. The best part? You can adjust the seasoning to suit your taste, whether you like things spicy, herby, or just classic.

Also, start small with batch sizes. When I first began, I would make a smaller portion just to get a feel for how the air fryer works. If it's your first time cooking a particular food, you may want to keep things simple and not overstuff the basket. That way, your food cooks evenly and you can see how the texture and taste come out.

BUILD YOUR CONFIDENCE

As you start seeing how quickly and easily your food crisps up, your confidence will grow. That initial hesitation will turn into excitement as you realize how little effort it takes to make meals that taste just as good (if not better) than deep-fried versions. Plus, cooking in the air fryer is cleaner and healthier—two big wins.

It's all about trial and error. Don't be afraid to adjust the temperature or cooking time a little based on your results. Air fryers can vary in how they cook, so don't be discouraged if it takes a little tweaking to get everything perfect. If you burn something, laugh it off and try again. It's part of the process.

EMBRACE MEAL PLANNING

One of the best ways to stick to air fryer recipes is by incorporating them into your regular meal planning. When you plan ahead, it's easier to make cooking with the air fryer a habit, rather than a one-time experiment. Planning your meals around the air fryer helps you get the most out of it—and believe me, you'll start to wonder how you ever lived without it.

Take some time each week to sit down and think about what you want to cook. Pick out a few recipes from this book (or others!) that excite you. Don't overcomplicate things—keep it realistic. You don't need a seven-course meal for every day of the week. Plan for a few air fryer-friendly meals and leave room for flexibility. One of the joys of air fryer cooking is how quickly you can whip up meals, so even on busy days, you'll have something satisfying ready to go.

MAKE IT A HABIT

Like any new skill, sticking to air fryer recipes is about creating consistency. Start by setting small goals. Maybe you aim to cook one air fryer meal a week. Once that feels natural, increase it to two or three. Over time, you'll find yourself using your air fryer more frequently. It becomes part of your routine, and before you know it, you'll be experimenting with different ingredients, trying new cooking techniques, and getting more creative with your meals.

If you ever feel like you're falling off track, it's okay. Life gets busy, and cooking can feel overwhelming at times. When that happens, remind yourself why you started. The air fryer is a tool to make your life easier, not harder. Don't beat yourself up for not using it every single day. Just pick up where you left off and enjoy the journey.

MIX THINGS UP

As you get more comfortable with air fryer cooking, don't be afraid to mix things up. This is the fun part! Try new ingredients and explore different types of cuisines. Air fryers can handle so much more than just fries and chicken—think crispy veggies, baked goods, and even quick desserts.

Get creative with seasoning blends and marinades. You can make everything from crispy tofu to roasted potatoes to air fryer pizzas. The possibilities are endless, and the more you experiment, the more you'll realize how versatile the air fryer really is.

If you find a recipe that works well, write it down or bookmark it. Soon, you'll have your own collection of go-to air fryer recipes that you can fall back on when you're in a rush or looking for inspiration.

CELEBRATE YOUR WINS

Lastly, remember to celebrate your successes. Did your first batch of crispy chicken come out perfect? High five! Is your air fryer sweet potato fries recipe a hit with the family? That's a win. Every time you nail a recipe or feel like you've mastered a new technique, take a moment to pat yourself on the back. Cooking is a journey, and it's the small victories that keep you motivated.

So, there you have it! Starting and sticking to air fryer recipes isn't about perfection—it's about making cooking easier, healthier, and more fun. Take it slow, enjoy the process, and let your air fryer become an essential tool in your kitchen. Trust me, once you get the hang of it, you won't want to cook any other way.

Are you ready to begin? Let's move on to some of the easiest and most delicious air fryer recipes you can try right away.

QUESTION

What's the first recipe you're excited to try in your air fryer, and why do you think it will be a game-changer for your cooking routine?

Have you ever found yourself hesitating to use a kitchen gadget because it felt too complicated? How do you think the simplicity of the air fryer could change your approach to cooking?

How do you usually plan your meals for the week? Can you imagine how easy it would be to add a few air fryer-friendly dishes to your menu?

What's one food you've always wanted to cook in a healthier way, but have been hesitant to try? How do you think the air fryer could help make that a reality?

What's the most challenging part of starting a new cooking habit for you, and what would it take for you to make the air fryer a consistent part of your routine?

HOW TO START AND STICK TO CRISPY RECIPES

To maintain a healthy lifestyle with air fryer cooking, the focus is on foods that are nutritious, low in unhealthy fats, and rich in natural flavors. Using the air fryer allows you to enjoy crispy, flavorful dishes with less oil, making it easier to make healthier food choices. Here's a breakdown of foods to eat and those to avoid for a healthier diet based on the principles of air fryer cooking:

FOODS TO EAT FOR BETTER HEALTH

Lean Proteins:

- **Chicken breast**: Air frying chicken breast is a great way to achieve a crispy texture without excess oil. Choose skinless, boneless options for a leaner meal.
- **Fish**: Fish like salmon, cod, and tilapia cook wonderfully in the air fryer. They are rich in omega-3 fatty acids and other nutrients that support heart health.
- **Tofu and Tempeh**: These plant-based proteins can be air-fried to crispy perfection. Tofu and tempeh are excellent sources of protein and can be marinated for added flavor.
- **Turkey**: Lean turkey, such as turkey breast or ground turkey, is a great source of protein and can be air-fried into healthy, crispy options like turkey burgers or meatballs.

Vegetables:

- **Broccoli**: Air-fried broccoli comes out crispy and caramelized without needing a lot of oil. It's full of vitamins, minerals, and fiber, making it a perfect side dish.
- **Cauliflower**: Cauliflower can be air-fried into crispy bites, or you can make cauliflower wings as a healthy alternative to deep-fried options.
- **Sweet Potatoes**: Air frying sweet potato fries or wedges is a great way to keep them healthy. They're packed with vitamins A and C, as well as fiber.
- **Zucchini**: Zucchini can be air-fried into crispy "fries" or used in fritters. It's low in calories and high in antioxidants.

Whole Grains:

- **Quinoa**: A great source of plant-based protein and fiber, quinoa can be made into air-fried veggie patties or incorporated into a variety of dishes for a healthy side.
- **Brown Rice**: Though not typically air-fried, you can use the air fryer to prep ingredients for stir-fries that feature brown rice, which is a more nutritious option compared to white rice.

Nuts and Seeds:

- **Almonds, walnuts, sunflower seeds**: You can use the air fryer to toast nuts and seeds, enhancing their flavor while keeping them healthy. Just be cautious of portion sizes since they are calorie-dense.

Healthy Fats:

- **Avocados**: Air frying avocado slices can add a crispy texture without overloading on unhealthy fats. Avocados are a source of heart-healthy monounsaturated fats.
- **Olive Oil**: If you use oil, opt for heart-healthy olive oil or avocado oil. A light spray or brush is all you need when using the air fryer, which keeps fat intake lower compared to deep frying.

FOODS TO AVOID (OR EAT IN MODERATION):

Processed Meats:

- **Bacon**: While bacon can be cooked in the air fryer and come out crispy, it's high in saturated fats and sodium, which are not great for heart health when consumed in excess.
- **Sausages and Hot Dogs**: These processed meats are often loaded with unhealthy fats, sodium, and preservatives. They should be eaten sparingly or swapped with leaner alternatives like turkey sausage.

Refined Carbohydrates:

- **White Bread**: While air-frying breaded items is possible, refined carbs like white bread or white pasta lack the nutritional value of whole grains. Instead, opt for whole-wheat options that are higher in fiber and nutrients.
- **White Rice**: As mentioned, white rice is less nutritious than brown rice, quinoa, or other whole grains. It has a higher glycemic index, which can lead to spikes in blood sugar.

Pre-Packaged Fried Foods:

- **Frozen French Fries**: Many pre-packaged frozen fries are deep-fried in unhealthy oils before being frozen. Even though you can air fry them, they often contain preservatives and unhealthy trans fats. It's better to make your own fries with fresh, unprocessed potatoes.
- **Frozen Breaded Snacks**: Many pre-breaded frozen foods, like nuggets or fish sticks, are loaded with refined flour, sugars, and unhealthy fats. Opt for homemade alternatives that are more nutrient-dense and free from additives.

Sugary Snacks and Sweets:

- **Dessert Baked Goods**: While you can use the air fryer to make cakes, cookies, and pies, it's important to keep these in moderation. These foods are often high in sugar and unhealthy fats, which can contribute to weight gain and other health issues if consumed too frequently.
- **Chips and Processed Snacks**: Whether you're air-frying potato chips or pre-packaged snack foods, they're often high in sodium, unhealthy fats, and preservatives. Opt for healthier snacks like air-fried veggies or homemade popcorn without butter.

Excessive Use of Oil:

- **Deep-fried Foods**: While the air fryer requires significantly less oil than deep frying, it's still possible to overdo it with oil. Overusing oil—even healthy ones—can still lead to higher calorie consumption, which can impact your health goals. Use oil sparingly for that crispy finish, and avoid dousing foods with excess oil.

KEY TIPS FOR HEALTHY AIR FRYER COOKING:

- **Control Portion Sizes**: Even with healthier foods, portion control is crucial for maintaining a balanced diet. The air fryer can cook foods quickly, but be mindful of how much you're preparing to avoid overeating.
- **Focus on Fresh Ingredients**: Whenever possible, choose fresh, whole foods over processed or packaged items. The more natural the ingredients, the healthier the meal.
- **Experiment with Seasoning**: Use herbs, spices, and citrus to enhance the flavor of your dishes without adding unnecessary salt or sugar. The air fryer will help bring out the natural flavors of your ingredients.
- **Avoid Overuse of Sauces**: Many sauces, especially store-bought ones, can be high in sugar and sodium. Consider making your own sauces with healthier ingredients like olive oil, lemon, and fresh herbs.

By choosing the right foods and using the air fryer to cook in a healthier way, you can create delicious, nutritious meals that support a well-balanced lifestyle. Enjoy the crispiness and flavors while staying mindful of what's going into your body!

QUESTION

What is the main benefit of using the air fryer for cooking?

A) It uses a lot of oil to make food crispy.

B) It helps you achieve a crispy texture with little to no oil.

C) It is only suitable for frying unhealthy foods.

D) It requires long cooking times for best results.

Which of the following foods is considered a healthier option for air frying?

A) Processed sausage

B) White bread

C) Sweet potatoes

D) Frozen French fries

Which of these foods should be avoided or eaten in moderation for a healthier air fryer diet?

A) Lean chicken breast

B) Frozen breaded snacks

C) Fresh vegetables

D) Salmon

Answer: B) It helps you achieve a crispy texture with little to no oil.

Answer: C) Sweet potatoes

Answer: B) Frozen breaded snacks

MEAL PLANNING FOR BEGINNER AIR FRYER RECIPES

Meal planning can be a game-changer, especially when you're starting out with air fryer recipes. By organizing your meals in advance, you can save time, reduce stress, and ensure you're sticking to healthier, more balanced options. For air fryer beginners, the key is to start simple and gradually build your confidence with new recipes. Here's a step-by-step guide to help you get started with meal planning for air fryer recipes.

STEP 1: UNDERSTAND YOUR AIR FRYER'S CAPABILITIES

Before diving into meal planning, it's important to understand the limitations and strengths of your air fryer. The air fryer works best for dishes that need to be crispy or browned, such as vegetables, proteins, and snacks. While it can handle a variety of dishes, it's ideal for cooking smaller portions, so keep that in mind when planning your meals. Additionally, many air fryers have preset cooking functions, so learning how these work for basic items like fries, chicken, and fish can help you get started quickly.

STEP 2: KEEP IT SIMPLE AT FIRST

As a beginner, try not to overwhelm yourself with complicated recipes. Stick to a few basic, easy-to-make meals that you enjoy and can prepare with minimal steps. Here's an example of a simple air fryer meal plan for the week:

- **Breakfast**: Air fryer scrambled eggs or air fryer avocado toast. You can add a side of air-fried bacon or potatoes for extra flavor.
- **Lunch**: Air fryer chicken tenders or a veggie wrap with air-fried sweet potato fries.
- **Dinner**: Air-fried salmon with roasted Brussels sprouts or a simple air fryer stir-fry with chicken and vegetables.

These meals are easy to prep, and they will help you get familiar with your air fryer while still keeping your diet balanced.

STEP 3: CREATE A BALANCED MEAL PLAN

When meal planning, aim for a balance of protein, healthy fats, and vegetables. The air fryer is excellent for cooking lean proteins like chicken, fish, and turkey, as well as vegetables like broccoli, zucchini, and sweet potatoes.

Example of a Balanced Air Fryer Meal Plan:

- **Day 1:**
    - **Breakfast**: Air-fried egg muffins with veggies
    - **Lunch**: Air-fried chicken breast with a side of roasted cauliflower and a quinoa salad
    - **Dinner**: Air-fried salmon with a simple side of roasted sweet potatoes and steamed green beans
- **Day 2:**
    - **Breakfast**: Air-fried avocado slices with whole-grain toast
    - **Lunch**: Air-fried turkey meatballs with a side of air-fried vegetables
    - **Dinner**: Air-fried shrimp tacos with cabbage slaw and homemade salsa

By including a mix of lean proteins, veggies, and whole grains, you'll be able to enjoy flavorful meals that are healthy and easy to make in the air fryer.

STEP 4: PREP INGREDIENTS IN ADVANCE

To make your week go smoothly, try doing some meal prep. This could mean chopping vegetables, marinating proteins, or portioning out snacks and sides. For example, you can prep the following:

- **Vegetables**: Pre-chop or slice vegetables like zucchini, bell peppers, and carrots. Store them in an airtight container, ready to be tossed into the air fryer.
- **Proteins**: Marinate chicken or tofu the night before. You can also batch cook chicken tenders or meatballs in the air fryer and use them in multiple meals throughout the week.
- **Snacks**: Consider making air fryer snacks, such as roasted chickpeas, veggie chips, or air-fried nuts, which can be prepped in advance and eaten throughout the week.

By having ingredients ready to go, you'll reduce cooking time and avoid the temptation to order takeout or rely on unhealthy options.

STEP 5: KEEP A SHOPPING LIST HANDY

Meal planning is only as effective as your grocery shopping. Make a shopping list based on your planned meals for the week. Include the essential items like vegetables, lean proteins, whole grains, and healthy fats. Here's an example shopping list for an air fryer-focused meal plan:

- **Proteins**: Chicken breasts, salmon, turkey meatballs, eggs
- **Vegetables**: Sweet potatoes, zucchini, broccoli, Brussels sprouts, cauliflower
- **Whole Grains**: Quinoa, brown rice, whole-grain bread
- **Healthy Fats**: Avocados, olive oil, nuts
- **Seasonings**: Salt, pepper, garlic powder, paprika, lemon juice

By keeping your shopping list focused on the ingredients you'll use in your air fryer recipes, you'll avoid unnecessary purchases and stay on track with your healthy eating goals.

STEP 6: EXPERIMENT WITH SIMPLE RECIPES

Once you've got the basics down, it's time to experiment. As you become more comfortable with your air fryer, try new recipes and add variety to your meal plan. Start with one or two new recipes each week, and soon you'll feel confident adapting them to your tastes.

For example:

- Try air-frying veggies with different seasoning combinations (garlic and lemon, paprika and cumin, etc.).
- Explore making healthier air fryer snacks, like air-fried kale chips or homemade sweet potato fries.
- Experiment with cooking different types of protein—try air-fried tofu or turkey burgers alongside your usual chicken or fish.

STEP 7: BE FLEXIBLE AND ADJUST

Don't stress if your meal plan doesn't go exactly as expected. Life happens, and sometimes schedules change or you may not feel like eating what you planned. The beauty of air frying is that it's quick and flexible, so if you need to switch up your plan, you can do so without a lot of hassle. If you're in a rush, consider having an easy backup plan, like air fryer veggie burgers or frozen fish fillets that you can quickly air fry and serve with a side salad.

STEP 8: ENJOY THE PROCESS

Meal planning should feel like a fun, rewarding activity—not a chore. Embrace the creativity that air frying brings, and don't be afraid to try new combinations of ingredients. The more you cook with the air fryer, the more you'll love the convenience, speed, and crispy results it delivers.

CONCLUSION

Meal planning with the air fryer is a great way to set yourself up for success. By starting simple, preparing ingredients ahead of time, and focusing on balanced meals, you'll be able to enjoy a wide variety of healthy, tasty dishes without spending hours in the kitchen. The air fryer makes cooking easier and more enjoyable—so take the leap and start meal planning today!

7-DAY AIR FRYER RECIPE MEAL PLAN

Here's a well-rounded, healthy 7-day meal plan with simple and delicious air fryer recipes for breakfast, lunch, and dinner. This plan focuses on lean proteins, vegetables, and wholesome ingredients that work perfectly with the air fryer. You can tweak the seasonings and ingredients to suit your taste

Day 1:

Breakfast: Air-Fried Avocado Toast

- **Ingredients**: Whole grain bread, 1 ripe avocado, lemon juice, salt, pepper, chili flakes (optional)
- **Instructions**: Toast the bread in the air fryer at 400°F for about 3 minutes. Mash the avocado with lemon juice, salt, and pepper. Spread over the toasted bread. Top with chili flakes for extra flavor.

Lunch: Air-Fried Chicken Tenders with Sweet Potato Fries

- **Ingredients**: 2 chicken breasts, bread crumbs, egg, garlic powder, paprika, salt, pepper, 1 sweet potato, olive oil
- **Instructions**: Coat the chicken strips in egg, then dip in seasoned bread crumbs. Air fry at 380°F for 10–12 minutes. For fries, cut sweet potato into wedges, season, and air fry at 400°F for 15 minutes, flipping halfway.

Dinner: Air-Fried Salmon with Roasted Brussels Sprouts

- **Ingredients**: 2 salmon fillets, olive oil, lemon, garlic, Brussels sprouts, salt, pepper
- **Instructions**: Season salmon with olive oil, lemon juice, garlic, salt, and pepper. Air fry at 375°F for 10 minutes. For Brussels sprouts, cut in half, season, and air fry at 400°F for 15 minutes.

Day 2:

Breakfast: Air-Fried Breakfast Burrito

- **Ingredients**: 1 whole-wheat tortilla, scrambled eggs, black beans, avocado, salsa, cheese

- **Instructions**: Fill the tortilla with scrambled eggs, black beans, cheese, and avocado. Wrap it tightly and air fry at 375°F for 5-7 minutes until crispy.

Lunch: **Air-Fried Turkey Meatballs with Zucchini Noodles**

- **Ingredients**: Ground turkey, breadcrumbs, egg, garlic, oregano, zucchini
- **Instructions**: Form turkey meatballs and air fry at 375°F for 10–12 minutes. For the zucchini noodles, spiralize the zucchini and sauté briefly in a pan or air fry at 375°F for 5 minutes.

Dinner: **Air-Fried Chicken Fajitas**

- **Ingredients**: 2 chicken breasts, bell peppers, onions, fajita seasoning, tortillas
- **Instructions**: Slice chicken, peppers, and onions. Toss with fajita seasoning. Air fry at 400°F for 10–12 minutes. Serve in tortillas with toppings like sour cream and salsa.

Day 3:

Breakfast: **Air-Fried Egg Muffins**

- **Ingredients**: Eggs, spinach, tomatoes, cheese, salt, pepper
- **Instructions**: Whisk the eggs and pour into silicone muffin cups. Add spinach, tomatoes, cheese, and seasoning. Air fry at 375°F for 10 minutes.

Lunch: **Air-Fried Chicken Caesar Salad**

- **Ingredients**: 2 chicken breasts, romaine lettuce, croutons, Caesar dressing, parmesan
- **Instructions**: Coat chicken breasts with olive oil, salt, and pepper. Air fry at 375°F for 10–12 minutes. Slice and serve on top of romaine lettuce with croutons, dressing, and parmesan.

Dinner: **Air-Fried Shrimp Tacos**

- **Ingredients**: Shrimp, taco seasoning, tortillas, cabbage, lime, salsa
- **Instructions**: Toss shrimp in taco seasoning and air fry at 375°F for 6-8 minutes. Serve in tortillas with shredded cabbage, salsa, and a squeeze of lime.

Day 4:

Breakfast: **Air-Fried Banana Oatmeal Bites**

- **Ingredients**: 1 ripe banana, oats, egg, cinnamon
- **Instructions**: Mash the banana and mix with oats, egg, and cinnamon. Scoop into muffin cups and air fry at 375°F for 8–10 minutes.

Lunch: **Air-Fried Veggie Burger with Sweet Potato Fries**

- **Ingredients**: Veggie burger patty, whole-grain bun, lettuce, tomato, avocado, 1 sweet potato
- **Instructions**: Air fry the veggie burger patty at 375°F for 6–8 minutes. For fries, cut sweet potato into wedges, season, and air fry at 400°F for 15 minutes.

Dinner: **Air-Fried Chicken Thighs with Cauliflower Rice**

- **Ingredients**: Bone-in chicken thighs, olive oil, garlic, paprika, cauliflower rice
- **Instructions**: Season chicken thighs and air fry at 380°F for 25 minutes. For cauliflower rice, sauté in a pan or air fry for 8–10 minutes at 375°F.

Day 5:

Breakfast: **Air-Fried Apple Chips**

- **Ingredients**: 1 apple, cinnamon
- **Instructions**: Slice apple thinly, sprinkle with cinnamon, and air fry at 350°F for 8-10 minutes, flipping halfway through.

Lunch: **Air-Fried Chicken Salad Wrap**

- **Ingredients**: Grilled chicken breast, spinach, avocado, tomatoes, whole-wheat wrap
- **Instructions**: Slice grilled chicken and layer with spinach, avocado, and tomatoes in the wrap. Serve with a side of air-fried veggie chips.

Dinner: **Air-Fried Tilapia with Roasted Asparagus**

- **Ingredients**: Tilapia fillets, olive oil, lemon, asparagus
- **Instructions**: Season tilapia fillets with olive oil, lemon, salt, and pepper, and air fry at 375°F for 8-10 minutes. Roast asparagus in the air fryer at 400°F for 8–10 minutes.

Day 6:

Breakfast: Air-Fried French Toast Sticks

- **Ingredients**: Whole grain bread, eggs, cinnamon, vanilla, maple syrup
- **Instructions**: Dip bread slices in egg mixture with cinnamon and vanilla. Air fry at 375°F for 6-8 minutes until golden and crispy. Serve with maple syrup.

Lunch: Air-Fried Veggie Fritters

- **Ingredients**: Zucchini, carrot, egg, flour, breadcrumbs, garlic powder
- **Instructions**: Grate zucchini and carrot, mix with egg, flour, breadcrumbs, and seasonings. Form into patties and air fry at 375°F for 8–10 minutes.

Dinner: Air-Fried Steak with Roasted Potatoes

- **Ingredients**: Steak, garlic, rosemary, olive oil, potatoes
- **Instructions**: Season steak with garlic and rosemary, and air fry at 400°F for 8-10 minutes for medium-rare. For potatoes, cut into wedges, season, and air fry at 400°F for 15 minutes.

Day 7:

Breakfast: Air-Fried Breakfast Quesadilla

- **Ingredients**: Whole wheat tortilla, scrambled eggs, cheese, salsa
- **Instructions**: Fill tortilla with scrambled eggs and cheese, fold, and air fry at 375°F for 5-7 minutes until crispy.

Lunch: Air-Fried Falafel with Tahini Sauce

- **Ingredients**: Canned chickpeas, garlic, parsley, cumin, tahini

- **Instructions**: Blend chickpeas, garlic, parsley, cumin, and salt to form a dough. Shape into balls and air fry at 375°F for 10–12 minutes. Serve with tahini sauce.

Dinner: **Air-Fried Chicken Parmesan with Zucchini Noodles**

- **Ingredients**: Chicken breast, breadcrumbs, marinara sauce, mozzarella, zucchini
- **Instructions**: Coat chicken in breadcrumbs, air fry at 375°F for 10–12 minutes. Top with marinara and mozzarella and air fry for 3–5 more minutes. Serve with zucchini noodles sautéed in olive oil.

Tips for Success:

- **Batch Cooking**: If you're short on time, batch cook your proteins or sides, like chicken or sweet potatoes, to use in multiple meals throughout the week.
- **Adjust Cooking Times**: Air fryers vary in temperature, so keep an eye on your food and adjust cooking times accordingly.
- **Prep in Advance**: Pre-cut veggies or marinate meats ahead of time to make cooking easier during the week.

This 7-day meal plan offers a diverse range of air fryer recipes that are easy to follow, nutritious, and delicious. Enjoy the crispy, healthier meals without all the oil and mess!

7 COMPREHENSIVE AIR FRYER BREAKFAST RECIPES

Here are 7 nutritious and delicious air fryer breakfast recipes. These recipes are designed to be quick, easy, and customizable to your tastes while providing a great start to your day. Each recipe includes ingredients, instructions, prep and cook time, servings, and nutritional information.

Air Fryer Avocado Toast

Ingredients:

- 2 slices whole-grain bread
- 1 ripe avocado
- 1 tablespoon lemon juice
- Salt and pepper to taste
- Red chili flakes (optional)

Instructions:

1. Preheat your air fryer to 400°F.
2. Toast the bread in the air fryer for about 3-4 minutes until crispy.
3. While the bread is toasting, mash the avocado with lemon juice, salt, and pepper.
4. Spread the mashed avocado evenly over the toasted bread.
5. Optionally, sprinkle chili flakes for some heat.

Cooking Time: 3-4 minutes
Prep Time: 5 minutes
Serving: 1-2 servings

Nutritional Information (per serving):

- Calories: 270 kcal
- Protein: 6g
- Carbs: 30g
- Fat: 16g
- Fiber: 10g
- Sodium: 300mg

Air Fryer reakfast Burrito

Ingredients:

- 1 whole-wheat tortilla
- 2 scrambled eggs
- 1/4 cup black beans (rinsed and drained)
- 1/4 avocado, sliced
- 2 tablespoons salsa
- 2 tablespoons shredded cheese

Instructions:

1. Scramble the eggs in a pan or microwave.
2. Lay the tortilla flat and fill it with scrambled eggs, black beans, avocado slices, salsa, and shredded cheese.
3. Roll up the tortilla tightly into a burrito shape.
4. Place the burrito in the air fryer basket and air fry at 375°F for 5-7 minutes until golden and crispy.

Cooking Time: 5-7 minutes
Prep Time: 10 minutes
Serving: 1 serving

Nutritional Information (per serving):

- Calories: 390 kcal
- Protein: 17g
- Carbs: 43g
- Fat: 17g
- Fiber: 10g
- Sodium: 480mg

Air Fryer Egg Muffins

Ingredients:

- 4 large eggs
- 1/4 cup spinach, chopped
- 1/4 cup diced bell peppers
- 1/4 cup shredded cheese (optional)
- Salt and pepper to taste

Instructions:

1. Preheat your air fryer to 375°F.
2. Grease muffin cups or silicone molds with cooking spray.
3. Whisk the eggs in a bowl and add chopped spinach, bell peppers, cheese, salt, and pepper.
4. Pour the egg mixture into the muffin cups, filling each about 3/4 full.
5. Air fry for 10 minutes, or until eggs are set and lightly browned.

Cooking Time: 10 minutes

Prep Time: 5 minutes

Serving: 2 servings (2 muffins each)

Nutritional Information (per serving):

- Calories: 180 kcal
- Protein: 14g
- Carbs: 4g
- Fat: 14g
- Fiber: 1g
- Sodium: 250mg

Air Fryer Banana Oatmeal Bites

Ingredients:

- 1 ripe banana
- 1/2 cup rolled oats
- 1/2 teaspoon cinnamon
- 1 egg
- 1/2 teaspoon vanilla extract

Instructions:

1. Preheat the air fryer to 375°F.
2. Mash the ripe banana in a bowl.
3. Add oats, cinnamon, egg, and vanilla extract, mixing until combined.
4. Spoon out portions of the mixture and form them into small bite-sized balls or patties.
5. Air fry for 8-10 minutes until golden and slightly crispy on the outside.

Cooking Time: 8-10 minutes

Prep Time: 5 minutes

Serving: 2 servings (4-5 bites each)

Nutritional Information (per serving):

- Calories: 220 kcal
- Protein: 5g
- Carbs: 35g
- Fat: 7g
- Fiber: 4g
- Sodium: 40mg

Air Fryer French Toast Sticks

Ingredients:

- 2 slices whole-grain bread
- 1/4 cup milk
- 1 egg
- 1 teaspoon cinnamon
- 1/2 teaspoon vanilla extract
- Maple syrup for serving

Instructions:

1. Preheat the air fryer to 375°F.
2. In a bowl, whisk together milk, egg, cinnamon, and vanilla extract.
3. Cut the bread into 4 strips each.
4. Dip the bread strips into the egg mixture and coat evenly.
5. Place the strips in the air fryer basket and cook for 6-8 minutes, flipping halfway through.
6. Serve with maple syrup.

Cooking Time: 6-8 minutes
Prep Time: 5 minutes
Serving: 1-2 servings

Nutritional Information (per serving):

- Calories: 280 kcal
- Protein: 9g
- Carbs: 38g
- Fat: 10g
- Fiber: 5g
- Sodium: 300mg

Air Fryer Sweet Potato Hash

Ingredients:

- 1 medium sweet potato, diced
- 1/4 cup red bell pepper, diced
- 1/4 cup onion, diced
- 1 tablespoon olive oil
- 1/4 teaspoon paprika
- Salt and pepper to taste

Instructions:

1. Preheat the air fryer to 400°F.
2. Toss the diced sweet potato, bell pepper, and onion with olive oil, paprika, salt, and pepper.
3. Air fry for 15 minutes, shaking the basket halfway through to ensure even cooking.
4. Serve hot.

Cooking Time: 15 minutes
Prep Time: 5 minutes
Serving: 2 servings

Nutritional Information (per serving):

- Calories: 190 kcal
- Protein: 3g
- Carbs: 40g
- Fat: 5g
- Fiber: 6g
- Sodium: 150mg

Air Fryer Breakfast Quesadilla

Ingredients:

- 1 whole-wheat tortilla
- 2 scrambled eggs
- 1/4 cup shredded cheese
- 1/4 cup salsa
- 2 tablespoons diced avocado

Instructions:

1. Scramble the eggs and set aside.
2. Place the tortilla flat and add scrambled eggs, cheese, salsa, and avocado.
3. Fold the tortilla into a half-moon shape and place it in the air fryer basket.
4. Air fry at 375°F for 5-7 minutes, flipping halfway, until crispy and golden.

Cooking Time: 5-7 minutes
Prep Time: 10 minutes
Serving: 1 serving

Nutritional Information (per serving):

- Calories: 330 kcal
- Protein: 18g
- Carbs: 28g
- Fat: 18g
- Fiber: 7g
- Sodium: 580mg

These air fryer breakfast recipes are quick, flavorful, and provide a great start to your day. With their balance of proteins, healthy fats, and carbs, they will keep you energized and satisfied.

7 Comprehensive Air Fryer Lunch Recipes

Here are 7 delicious and nutritious air fryer lunch recipes that are easy to prepare and perfect for a satisfying midday meal. Each recipe includes ingredients, instructions, prep and cooking time, servings, and nutritional information.

Air Fryer Chicken Caesar Salad

Ingredients:

- 2 chicken breasts
- 1 tablespoon olive oil
- 1 teaspoon garlic powder
- 1 teaspoon paprika
- Salt and pepper to taste
- 4 cups romaine lettuce, chopped
- 1/4 cup Caesar dressing
- 1/4 cup croutons
- 2 tablespoons grated parmesan cheese

Instructions:

1. Preheat the air fryer to 375°F.
2. Rub chicken breasts with olive oil, garlic powder, paprika, salt, and pepper.
3. Air fry the chicken at 375°F for 10-12 minutes, flipping halfway through, until fully cooked and golden.
4. Slice the chicken into strips.
5. In a large bowl, toss the lettuce with Caesar dressing, croutons, and parmesan cheese.
6. Top with sliced chicken and serve.

Cooking Time: 10-12 minutes
Prep Time: 5 minutes
Serving: 2 servings

Nutritional Information (per serving):

- Calories: 400 kcal
- Protein: 38g
- Carbs: 14g
- Fat: 22g
- Fiber: 4g
- Sodium: 750mg

Air Fryer Turkey and Cheese Sandwich

Ingredients:

- 2 slices whole-grain bread
- 4 slices deli turkey
- 2 slices cheese (Swiss or cheddar)
- 1 tablespoon butter or olive oil
- 1/4 teaspoon garlic powder

Instructions:

1. Preheat the air fryer to 375°F.
2. Butter one side of each slice of bread and sprinkle with garlic powder.
3. Place one slice of cheese, turkey, and another slice of cheese between the bread slices (buttered side out).
4. Air fry the sandwich for 5-7 minutes, flipping halfway through, until golden and crispy.

Cooking Time: 5-7 minutes
Prep Time: 5 minutes
Serving: 1 sandwich

Nutritional Information (per serving):

- Calories: 350 kcal
- Protein: 30g
- Carbs: 30g
- Fat: 18g
- Fiber: 4g
- Sodium: 900mg

Air Fryer eggie Burger

Ingredients:

- 1 veggie burger patty (store-bought or homemade)
- 1 whole-grain burger bun
- Lettuce, tomato, and pickles for topping
- 1 tablespoon mustard or ketchup

Instructions:

1. Preheat the air fryer to 375°F.
2. Place the veggie burger patty in the air fryer basket and air fry for 8-10 minutes, flipping halfway through.
3. Toast the burger bun in the air fryer for 2-3 minutes.
4. Assemble the burger with the patty, lettuce, tomato, pickles, and your choice of mustard or ketchup.

Cooking Time: 10 minutes
Prep Time: 5 minutes
Serving: 1 burger

Nutritional Information (per serving):

- Calories: 280 kcal
- Protein: 14g
- Carbs: 38g
- Fat: 9g
- Fiber: 8g
- Sodium: 600mg

Air Fryer Chicken Tenders with Sweet Potato Fries

Ingredients:

- 2 chicken breasts, cut into strips
- 1/2 cup breadcrumbs
- 1 egg, beaten
- 1 tablespoon olive oil
- 1 medium sweet potato, cut into fries
- 1/2 teaspoon paprika
- Salt and pepper to taste

Instructions:

1. Preheat the air fryer to 375°F.
2. Dip the chicken strips in the beaten egg, then coat with breadcrumbs.
3. Air fry the chicken at 375°F for 8-10 minutes, flipping halfway through.
4. Toss the sweet potato fries with olive oil, paprika, salt, and pepper.
5. Air fry the fries at 400°F for 15 minutes, shaking halfway through.
6. Serve the chicken tenders with sweet potato fries on the side.

Cooking Time: 8-10 minutes (chicken) + 15 minutes (fries)
Prep Time: 10 minutes
Serving: 2 servings

Nutritional Information (per serving):

- Calories: 450 kcal
- Protein: 40g
- Carbs: 50g
- Fat: 14g
- Fiber: 8g
- Sodium: 600mg

Air Fryer Mediterranean Chicken Wrap

Ingredients:

- 1 chicken breast, cooked and sliced
- 1 whole-wheat wrap
- 1/4 cup hummus
- 1/4 cup cucumber, diced
- 1/4 cup cherry tomatoes, halved
- 1 tablespoon feta cheese, crumbled
- 1 tablespoon olive oil
- Salt and pepper to taste

Instructions:

1. Preheat the air fryer to 375°F.
2. Coat the chicken breast with olive oil, salt, and pepper, then air fry for 10-12 minutes, flipping halfway.
3. Lay the wrap flat and spread hummus in the center.
4. Layer with chicken, cucumber, tomatoes, and feta cheese.
5. Roll the wrap tightly and air fry for 3-4 minutes to seal the wrap and make it crispy.

Cooking Time: 10-12 minutes (chicken) + 3-4 minutes (wrap)
Prep Time: 10 minutes
Serving: 1 wrap

Nutritional Information (per serving):

- Calories: 400 kcal
- Protein: 35g
- Carbs: 30g
- Fat: 18g
- Fiber: 6g
- Sodium: 800mg

Air Fryer Grilled Cheese with Tomato Soup

Ingredients:

- 2 slices whole-grain bread
- 2 slices cheddar cheese
- 1 tablespoon butter
- 1 cup tomato soup (store-bought or homemade)

Instructions:

1. Preheat the air fryer to 375°F.
2. Butter one side of each slice of bread.
3. Place cheese between the slices of bread (buttered side out).
4. Air fry the sandwich for 5-7 minutes, flipping halfway through, until golden and crispy.
5. Heat the tomato soup in a pot or microwave.
6. Serve the grilled cheese with a bowl of tomato soup.

Cooking Time: 5-7 minutes (sandwich)
Prep Time: 5 minutes
Serving: 1 sandwich and soup

Nutritional Information (per serving):

- Calories: 450 kcal
- Protein: 20g
- Carbs: 42g
- Fat: 25g
- Fiber: 5g
- Sodium: 800mg

Air Fryer Falafel with Tahini Sauce

Ingredients:

- 1 cup canned chickpeas, drained and rinsed
- 2 tablespoons parsley, chopped
- 1 tablespoon onion, diced
- 2 cloves garlic, minced
- 1 tablespoon flour
- 1 teaspoon cumin
- Salt and pepper to taste
- 2 tablespoons tahini sauce

Instructions:

1. Preheat the air fryer to 375°F.
2. Blend the chickpeas, parsley, onion, garlic, flour, cumin, salt, and pepper in a food processor until smooth but slightly chunky.
3. Form the mixture into small balls or patties.
4. Place the falafel in the air fryer basket and air fry for 8-10 minutes, flipping halfway.
5. Drizzle with tahini sauce before serving.

Cooking Time: 8-10 minutes

Prep Time: 10 minutes

Serving: 2 servings (3-4 falafel each)

Nutritional Information (per serving):

- Calories: 250 kcal
- Protein: 10g
- Carbs: 30g
- Fat: 12g
- Fiber: 8g
- Sodium: 500mg

These air fryer lunch recipes offer a range of flavors and healthy ingredients to help you maintain energy throughout the day. They're quick, easy to prepare, and full of nutrients to support your active lifestyle!

7 COMPREHENSIVE AIR FRYER DINNER RECIPES

Here are 7 hearty and delicious air fryer dinner recipes that are perfect for a satisfying evening meal. Each recipe is simple to prepare and packed with nutrients. Each recipe includes ingredients, instructions, prep and cooking time, servings, and nutritional information.

Air Fryer Lemon Herb Chicken Thighs

Ingredients:

- 4 bone-in chicken thighs, skin-on
- 2 tablespoons olive oil
- 1 tablespoon lemon zest
- 2 tablespoons lemon juice
- 1 teaspoon garlic powder
- 1 teaspoon dried oregano
- Salt and pepper to taste

Instructions:

1. Preheat the air fryer to 400°F.
2. Pat the chicken thighs dry with a paper towel.
3. Rub the chicken thighs with olive oil, lemon zest, lemon juice, garlic powder, oregano, salt, and pepper.
4. Place the chicken thighs in the air fryer basket, skin-side down.
5. Air fry for 20-25 minutes, flipping halfway, until the internal temperature reaches 165°F and the skin is crispy.

Cooking Time: 20-25 minutes
Prep Time: 10 minutes
Serving: 4 servings

Nutritional Information (per serving):

- Calories: 300 kcal
- Protein: 27g
- Carbs: 3g
- Fat: 21g
- Fiber: 1g
- Sodium: 350mg

Air Fryer Salmon Fillets

Ingredients:

- 4 salmon fillets (about 4-6 oz each)
- 1 tablespoon olive oil
- 1 teaspoon garlic powder
- 1 teaspoon paprika
- 1/2 teaspoon lemon zest
- Salt and pepper to taste
- Fresh lemon wedges for serving

Instructions:

1. Preheat the air fryer to 400°F.
2. Rub the salmon fillets with olive oil and season with garlic powder, paprika, lemon zest, salt, and pepper.
3. Place the salmon fillets in the air fryer basket, skin-side down.
4. Air fry for 8-10 minutes, or until the salmon easily flakes with a fork.

Cooking Time: 8-10 minutes

Prep Time: 5 minutes

Serving: 4 servings

Nutritional Information (per serving):

- Calories: 270 kcal
- Protein: 23g
- Carbs: 1g
- Fat: 20g
- Fiber: 0g
- Sodium: 200mg

Air Fryer Stuffed Bell Peppers

Ingredients:

- 4 bell peppers (any color)
- 1/2 pound ground turkey or beef
- 1/2 cup cooked rice
- 1/2 cup black beans (canned, drained, and rinsed)
- 1/2 cup diced tomatoes
- 1/4 cup shredded cheese (cheddar or mozzarella)
- 1 teaspoon cumin
- Salt and pepper to taste

Instructions:

1. Preheat the air fryer to 375°F.
2. Cut the tops off the bell peppers and remove the seeds and ribs.
3. In a skillet, cook the ground turkey or beef over medium heat until browned. Add the cooked rice, black beans, diced tomatoes, cumin, salt, and pepper.
4. Stuff the bell peppers with the meat mixture, then top with shredded cheese.
5. Place the stuffed peppers in the air fryer basket and cook for 10-12 minutes, until the peppers are tender and the cheese is melted.

Cooking Time: 10-12 minutes
Prep Time: 10 minutes
Serving: 4 servings

Nutritional Information (per serving):

- Calories: 320 kcal
- Protein: 25g
- Carbs: 34g
- Fat: 12g
- Fiber: 7g
- Sodium: 500mg

Air Fryer Shrimp Scampi

Ingredients:

- 1 pound large shrimp, peeled and deveined
- 2 tablespoons olive oil
- 3 cloves garlic, minced
- 1 teaspoon lemon zest
- 1 tablespoon lemon juice
- 1/2 teaspoon paprika
- Salt and pepper to taste
- Fresh parsley for garnish

Instructions:

1. Preheat the air fryer to 400°F.
2. In a bowl, toss the shrimp with olive oil, garlic, lemon zest, lemon juice, paprika, salt, and pepper.
3. Place the shrimp in the air fryer basket in a single layer.
4. Air fry for 5-6 minutes, shaking the basket halfway through, until shrimp are pink and cooked through.
5. Garnish with fresh parsley and serve with pasta or a side salad.

Cooking Time: 5-6 minutes
Prep Time: 5 minutes
Serving: 4 servings

Nutritional Information (per serving):

- Calories: 220 kcal
- Protein: 25g
- Carbs: 3g
- Fat: 12g
- Fiber: 1g
- Sodium: 600mg

Air Fryer ucchini Fritters

Ingredients:

- 2 medium zucchinis, grated
- 1/4 cup all-purpose flour
- 1/4 cup breadcrumbs
- 1 egg
- 1/4 cup grated parmesan cheese
- 1/2 teaspoon garlic powder
- Salt and pepper to taste

Instructions:

1. Preheat the air fryer to 375°F.
2. Squeeze excess moisture out of the grated zucchini using a clean kitchen towel.
3. In a bowl, mix the zucchini, flour, breadcrumbs, egg, parmesan cheese, garlic powder, salt, and pepper.
4. Form the mixture into small fritters and place them in the air fryer basket.
5. Air fry for 10-12 minutes, flipping halfway through, until golden brown and crispy.

Cooking Time: 10-12 minutes
Prep Time: 10 minutes
Serving: 4 servings

Nutritional Information (per serving):

- Calories: 150 kcal
- Protein: 6g
- Carbs: 18g
- Fat: 7g
- Fiber: 3g
- Sodium: 350mg

Air Fryer Chicken Parmesan

Ingredients:

- 2 chicken breasts
- 1/2 cup breadcrumbs
- 1/4 cup grated parmesan cheese
- 1 egg, beaten
- 1 cup marinara sauce
- 1/2 cup shredded mozzarella cheese
- 1 tablespoon olive oil

Instructions:

1. Preheat the air fryer to 375°F.
2. Coat the chicken breasts with the egg, then dip them into a mixture of breadcrumbs and parmesan cheese.
3. Spray both sides of the chicken with olive oil and place them in the air fryer basket.
4. Air fry for 10-12 minutes, flipping halfway, until the chicken is cooked through and the coating is crispy.
5. Top the chicken with marinara sauce and shredded mozzarella cheese. Air fry for an additional 3-4 minutes, until the cheese is melted and bubbly.

Cooking Time: 15-16 minutes
Prep Time: 10 minutes
Serving: 2 servings

Nutritional Information (per serving):

- Calories: 400 kcal
- Protein: 38g
- Carbs: 18g
- Fat: 20g
- Fiber: 3g
- Sodium: 800mg

Air Fryer eriyaki Salmon Bowl

Ingredients:

- 2 salmon fillets
- 2 tablespoons teriyaki sauce
- 1 teaspoon sesame oil
- 1 tablespoon honey
- 1/2 cup cooked rice
- 1/4 cup steamed broccoli
- 1/4 cup sliced cucumber
- 1 tablespoon sesame seeds

Instructions:

1. Preheat the air fryer to 400°F.
2. Brush the salmon fillets with teriyaki sauce, sesame oil, and honey.
3. Place the salmon in the air fryer basket, skin-side down, and air fry for 8-10 minutes, or until the salmon easily flakes with a fork.
4. While the salmon is cooking, prepare the rice, steamed broccoli, and cucumber slices.
5. Assemble the bowl by placing the rice, broccoli, cucumber, and salmon in a bowl. Drizzle with extra teriyaki sauce and top with sesame seeds.

Cooking Time: 8-10 minutes
Prep Time: 10 minutes
Serving: 2 servings

Nutritional Information (per serving):

- Calories: 450 kcal
- Protein: 35g
- Carbs: 38g
- Fat: 18g
- Fiber: 6g
- Sodium: 850mg

These 7 air fryer diner recipes provide a range of flavors, from healthy seafood options to crispy, savory dishes. Whether you're in the mood for a light, protein-packed dinner or a heartier meal, these recipes are sure to satisfy!

CONCLUSION

As we wrap up this journey through "The Crisp & Simple Cookbook," we hope you feel inspired, empowered, and ready to dive into the world of air fryer cooking. This book was crafted to simplify your approach to savory meals, offering you a convenient way to create delicious and nutritious dishes without the hassle. By now, you have a solid foundation for understanding the principles of air frying, meal planning, and how to stick to a savory recipe lifestyle that is both rewarding and sustainable.

Throughout this cookbook, we've explored easy-to-follow recipes for every occasion, from breakfast to dinner, designed to make your life easier and your meals more exciting. We've covered everything from crispy chicken thighs to veggie-packed dishes, giving you the tools to enjoy satisfying meals that cater to a variety of tastes and preferences. Whether you're a beginner or a seasoned air fryer expert, each recipe is aimed at delivering a flavorful experience that will keep you coming back for more.

But beyond just the recipes, this cookbook is about fostering a lifestyle—one where healthy, home-cooked meals are a joy to prepare and share. With the air fryer as your trusty companion, meal planning becomes easier, cooking becomes faster, and cleaning up becomes simpler. You'll find yourself making nourishing meals more often, staying consistent, and feeling accomplished in the kitchen.

Remember, cooking is not just about following a set of instructions—it's about embracing the process, experimenting with flavors, and finding what works best for you. The key to success is consistency, creativity, and a little bit of joy in the kitchen. So, take the lessons you've learned here and let them inspire you to explore new possibilities, try out your own variations, and make air frying a fun and effortless part of your routine.

Whether you're cooking for yourself, your family, or entertaining friends, "The Crisp & Simple Cookbook" will be here to guide you every step of the way. We hope it becomes your go-to resource for savory meals, and that it sparks a newfound love for healthy, crispy, and simple air fryer recipes.

WEEKLY PLANNER

Fighting!

MONTH: **WEEK OF:**

MONDAY

TUESDAY

WEDNESDAY

THURSDAY

FRIDAY

SATURDAY

SUNDAY

NOTE:

WEEKLY PLANNER
Fighting!

MONTH: **WEEK OF:**

MONDAY	TUESDAY	WEDNESDAY

THURSDAY	FRIDAY	SATURDAY

SUNDAY	NOTE:

WEEKLY PLANNER
Fighting!

MONTH: **WEEK OF:**

MONDAY

TUESDAY

WEDNESDAY

THURSDAY

FRIDAY

SATURDAY

SUNDAY

NOTE:

WEEKLY PLANNER

Fighting!

MONTH: **WEEK OF:**

MONDAY

TUESDAY

WEDNESDAY

THURSDAY

FRIDAY

SATURDAY

SUNDAY

NOTE:

WEEKLY PLANNER

Fighting!

MONTH:

WEEK OF:

MONDAY

TUESDAY

WEDNESDAY

THURSDAY

FRIDAY

SATURDAY

SUNDAY

NOTE:

WEEKLY PLANNER

Fighting!

MONTH: **WEEK OF:**

MONDAY

TUESDAY

WEDNESDAY

THURSDAY

FRIDAY

SATURDAY

SUNDAY

NOTE:

WEEKLY PLANNER
Fighting!

MONTH: **WEEK OF:**

MONDAY

TUESDAY

WEDNESDAY

THURSDAY

FRIDAY

SATURDAY

SUNDAY

NOTE:

WEEKLY PLANNER
Fighting!

MONTH: **WEEK OF:**

MONDAY

TUESDAY

WEDNESDAY

THURSDAY

FRIDAY

SATURDAY

SUNDAY

NOTE:

WEEKLY PLANNER

Fighting!

MONTH: **WEEK OF:**

MONDAY

TUESDAY

WEDNESDAY

THURSDAY

FRIDAY

SATURDAY

SUNDAY

NOTE:

WEEKLY PLANNER
Fighting!

MONTH: **WEEK OF:**

MONDAY

TUESDAY

WEDNESDAY

THURSDAY

FRIDAY

SATURDAY

SUNDAY

NOTE:

Printed in Great Britain
by Amazon